080653L

Wonders of the Sea

Sea-grass Beds

Kimberley Jane Pryor

Smart Apple Media

This edition first published in 2008 in the United States of America by Smart Apple Media.

Smart Apple Media
2140 Howard Drive West
North Mankato, Minnesota 56003

First published in 2007 by
MACMILLAN EDUCATION AUSTRALIA PTY LTD
627 Chapel Street, South Yarra, Australia 3141

Visit our Web site at www.macmillan.com.au or go directly to www.macmillanlibrary.com.au

Associated companies and representatives throughout the world.

Library of Congress Cataloging-in-Publication Data

Pryor, Kimberley Jane.
   Sea-grass beds / by Kimberley Jane Pryor.
   p. cm. — (Wonders of the sea)
   Includes index.
   ISBN 978-1-59920-141-2
   1. Marine ecology—Juvenile literature. 2. Sea grasses—Ecology—Juvenile literature. I. Title.

   QH541.5.S3P79 2007
   577.7—dc22

                                                          2007004806

Edited by Erin Richards
Text and cover design by Christine Deering
Page layout by Domenic Lauricella
Photo research by Legend Images

Printed in U.S.

Acknowledgements
The author and the publisher are grateful to the following for permission to reproduce copyright material:

Cover photograph: Zebra fish feeding on a seagrass bed courtesy of G. Saueracker/Lochman Transparencies.

© Suzanne Long/Alamy, p. 17; © Visual&Written SL/Alamy, p. 12 (top); Jürgen Freund/AUSCAPE, p. 18; Karen Gowlett-Holmes AUSCAPE, p. 15; John Lewis/AUSCAPE, pp. 16, 22; © Craig Allen, Australian Fisheries Management Authority, p. 20; Coo-ee Picture Library, p. 13 (top); Dreamstime, pp. 3, 13 (bottom), 19, 21, 30; Getty Images, p. 23; Eva Boogaard/Lochman Transparencies, pp. 5, 6; Clay Bryce/Lochman Transparencies, pp. 7, 8, 9, 12 (bottom); John Butler/Lochman Transparencies, p. 26; G. Saueracker/Lochman Transparencies, pp. 1, 24; Alex Steffe/Lochman Transparencies,
p. 11; Geoff Taylor/Lochman Transparencies, p. 25; NOAA, p. 28; NASA Goddard Space Flight Center, p. 4; National Park Service/Biscayne National Park, p. 29; Photodisc, p. 27 (left); Photolibrary.com/OSF/Tobias Bernhard, p. 27 (right); Photolibrary.com/Photo Researchers Inc, pp. 10, 14.

For Nick, Thomas and Ashley
– Kimberley Jane Pryor

Contents

Glossary words
When a word is printed in **bold**, you can look up its meaning in the glossary on page 31.

The sea

The sea is a very large area of salty water. It covers most of Earth's surface.

The blue part of Earth is the sea.

The sea has many different **habitats**. Sea-grass beds are habitats that are found in shallow water close to land.

Sea-grass beds are found in calm, shallow water.

Sea-grass beds

Sea-grass beds are areas where sea grass grows. Sea grass is grass that grows in salty water.

Some sea grass has oval-shaped leaves.

Sea-grass beds are full of life. They provide food and shelter for many different plants and animals.

Bobtail squid find shelter in sea-grass beds.

Plants

Sea grass is a plant that can grow in sand and mud. Some form very large beds, which are called sea-grass meadows.

Sea-grass meadows look like the green lawns you see on land.

Sea grass has stems and leaves. Small plants, called seaweed, sometimes grow on them.

Seaweed

Small seaweed grows on hard surfaces, such as sea-grass leaves.

Animals

Different kinds of animals live in sea-grass beds. Clams and sea worms burrow into the sand and mud. Crabs scurry across the sea floor.

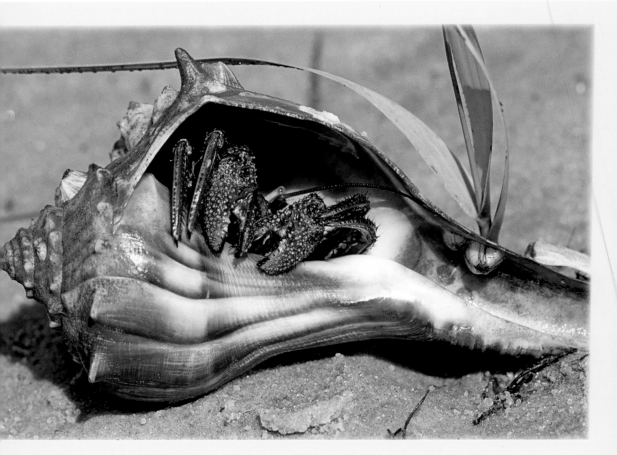

The stareye hermit crab finds an empty shell to live in.

Prawns and fish swim among the sea grass.
Sea snails crawl along the stems and leaves.
Dugongs, manatees, and turtles swim by.

Prawns search for food on the sea floor at night.

Where animals live

In a sea-grass bed, each kind of animal has a special place to live.

Blue jellyfish float near the surface of the sea.

Sand dollars are found on the sea floor.

Ospreys swoop for fish near the surface of the sea.

Leatherjackets swim among the sea grass.

Survival

To survive in a sea-grass bed, animals need to find and eat food. Sea horses use their long snouts to suck up tiny animals to eat.

Long snouts for sucking up food

Sea horses hold onto the sea grass with their tails.

Animals also need to protect themselves from **predators**. Some animals use their colors and others use their body parts.

Green color to match sea grass

Long body to look like a sea-grass leaf

Pipefish use their color and shape to hide from predators.

Small animals

Many small animals live in sea-grass beds. Crabs and sea stars move along the sea floor.

This decorator crab is wearing a sea-grass disguise to hide from predators.

Sea worms and sea snails crawl over sea-grass plants looking for food. Sea urchins feed on sea-grass leaves.

Sea urchins eat the leaves of sea grass.

Large animals

Large animals, such as dugongs, manatees, and turtles, live in sea-grass beds.

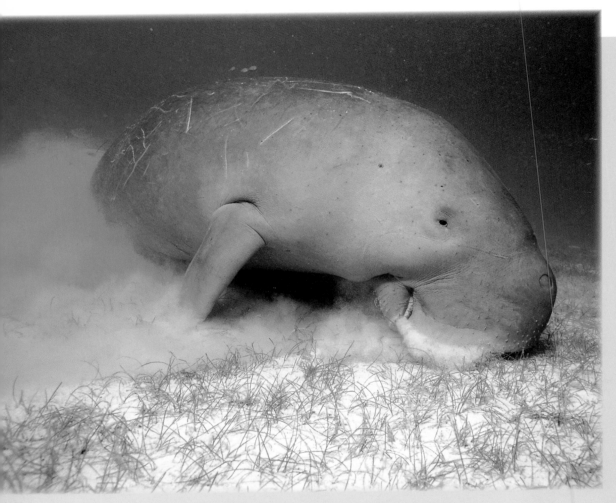

Dugongs are plant-eaters that eat sea grass.

Manatees live in rivers, **river mouths**, and shallow waters near the **shore**. They eat sea grass and many other water plants.

Manatees are found in shallow water.

Turtles eat sea grass, seaweed, and small animals such as jellyfish.

Green turtles use their flippers to move through the water.

Swans eat water plants. Their long necks help them reach the plants growing on the sea floor.

Black swans use their long necks to reach sea-grass plants to eat.

Fish

Many young fish live in sea-grass beds because they find food there. They can also hide from predators among the sea-grass leaves.

Barracudas sometimes hunt for fish in sea-grass beds.

Some fish leave sea-grass beds to live on coral reefs or in the open sea. Other fish, such as sea dragons, stay in sea-grass beds their whole lives.

Weedy sea dragons have leaf-like body parts to help them hide in sea grass.

Living together

Sometimes animals live together for protection. Some fish swim in a group, called a school. This makes it harder for a predator to choose and catch a fish.

Zebra fish often swim in schools.

Some animals survive by living with another kind of animal. Remoras are fish that attach themselves to large animals. They clean the animals and share their food.

Remoras clean the dugong as it swims along.

Food chain

Living things depend on other living things for food. This is called a food chain.

This is how a food chain works.

Plant

food for

This is a simple sea-grass bed food chain.

food for

Turtle grass makes its food using energy from the sun.

| **Plant-eating animal** | food for | **Animal-eating animal** |

food for

Turtle grass is food for green turtles.

Green turtles are food for tiger sharks.

Threats to sea-grass beds

Sea-grass beds can be **threatened** by natural events, such as storms. Big waves from hurricanes tear up sea grass. Heavy rain washes soil down rivers and onto sea-grass beds.

Storms, such as hurricanes, bring high winds and heavy rain.

Sea-grass beds are also threatened by people who:
- let raw **sewage** flow into the sea
- dig up sea grass with **dredges**
- tear through sea grass with boat propellers
- drag fishing nets along the sea floor

Boat propellers in shallow water can damage sea-grass beds.

Protecting sea-grass beds

We help protect sea-grass beds when we:

- stop raw sewage from flowing into the sea
- do not use dredges where there are seagrass beds
- only use boats in deep water
- keep fishing nets off the sea floor

Boats that are in deep water do not damage sea-grass beds.